At Stego Books, we are committed to unlock your child's greatest potential. We aspire to equip every child with entrepreneurial and imperative soft skills essential to be leaders of tomorrow through storytelling.

Our books are designed by education and entrepreneurship experts to instill entrepreneurial spirit from a young age effectively.

We inspire purposeful reading every day!

www.stegobooks.com | Instagram: @stegolearning

Ted Builds a Startup
Entrepreneurship
How You Can Be a Kidpreneur

"Hello, I'm Ted!" Ted is a diligent kid who loves gardening and fishing with his family on the weekends.

One day, Ted asks his father, "Hey Dad, I keep on hearing news about entrepreneurship and startups. What is entrepreneurship? How to build a startup?"

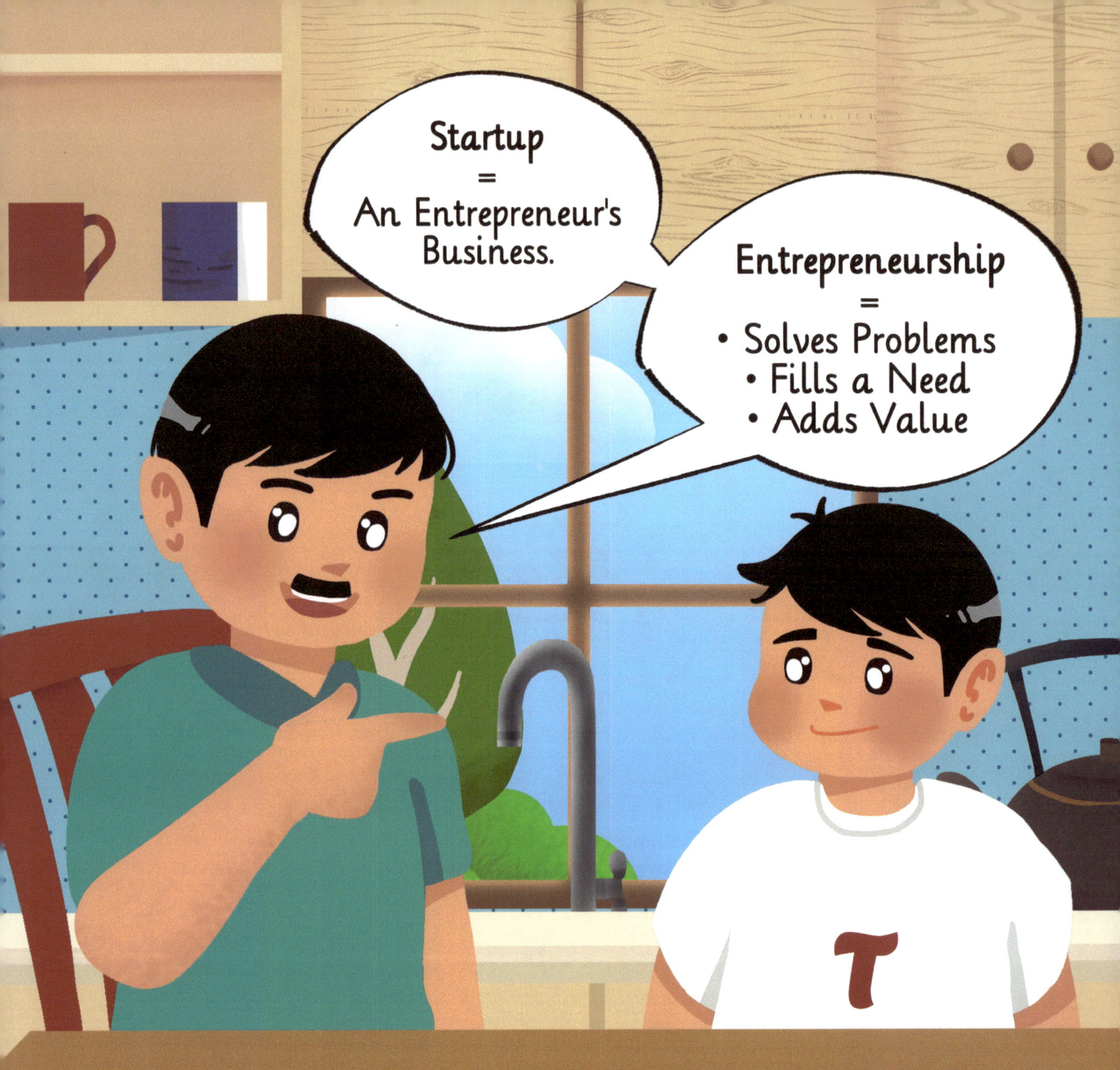

Dad responds, "Entrepreneurship is the act of setting up a business that solves problems, fills a need and adds value around us. An entrepreneur's business is a startup."

Dad continues, "To build a startup, you need an idea. You can generate an idea by thinking from these two things: problems and hobbies."

As Ted prepares to sleep, Ted thinks of his hobbies and problems around him. Ted's hobby is gardening; therefore, he wants to sell his homegrown fruits tomorrow. Will he be able to do it? Let's find out!

The next morning, Ted collects oranges and apples from his backyard. Eager to sell his fruits, Ted and his father begin walking to the river.

As Ted and his dad reach the river to fish, Ted begins asking the anglers nearby if they want to buy his fruits. None of them wants to buy his fruits.

Ted asks his dad why no one wants to buy his fruits. His dad replies, "Ted, selling goods from your hobby is not enough. One essential part of a startup is your product must fill a need."

With determination, Ted goes back to the anglers nearby and asks them what they need. Ted carefully notes down their needs.

As the day turns into night, Ted walks back home with his fruits unsold. Although Ted is sad, he does not give up. Ted is eager to fill the anglers' needs and build his startup.

At home, Ted examines the anglers' needs. Ted thinks, "What's easy to carry, cold, and sweet?" After a while, Ted shouts a brilliant idea, "Fruit popsicles!"

Ted immediately goes to the kitchen and creates fruit popsicles by juicing his fruits and freezing them. Ted is excited to fulfill the anglers' needs tomorrow.

The next morning, Ted and his dad go back fishing. As they reach the river, Ted approaches the anglers with his fruit popsicles.

Ted asks, "Do you want to buy a fruit popsicle for $10.00 each?" Unfortunately, the anglers decline as the fruit popsicles are too expensive.

Ted listens to the feedback and lowers his price to $5.00. The anglers love the new price and immediately purchase the fruit popsicles. Ted continues to sell all his fruit popsicles.

While having dinner, Ted proudly recounts his achievement. He is glad his product fits the anglers' needs. Ted realizes he can sell more popsicles, but he is unable to do it alone.

Mom says, "To build a startup, you need distributors. They are the people who help sell your products." Hence, Ted's mom suggests Ted to invite his friends, Angela and David to be his distributors.

After dinner, Ted calls Angela and David; he tells them about his startup. Ted is elated as Angela and David want to help him distribute his fruit popsicles!

The next day, Ted goes fishing with his family, Angela, and David. They are all eager to catch some fish and sell more fruit popsicles today!

With perseverance, Ted, Angela, and David move to different parts of the river and distribute more fruit popsicles.

With the help of social media, Angela and David distribute even more fruit popsicles by promoting them online. Ted's customers come to thank him for fulfilling their cold and sweet cravings on a sunny day.

Ted gives his fruit popsicles to his parents, Angela, and David. Ted says, "Thank you so much for teaching me how to build a startup!"

Ted learns in order to build a startup, he needs to solve a problem, fill a need, and add value. With the correct target market, pricing and distribution, Ted is able to build "Ted's Fruit Popsicles"!

As Ted, his parents, Angela, and David walk back home, they hold each other's hands with joy and happiness. They can't wait to build the next startup!

What problems do you see around you?

Thinking Time

What are your hobbies?

List Down Your Ideas!

Idea	Solves Problems	Fills a Need	Adds Value
Ted's Fruit Popsicles	✓	✓	✓

Design Your Own Stand!
Thinking
Time
Your
Photo

My Favorite Entrepreneur

Photo

Name:

Business:

Why I like this entrepreneur:

Entrepreneurship Affirmations

I am able to change the world.

I solve problems.

I provide a product or service that people need.

I am focused and resilient.

I build startups.

Spot the 5 Differences!

Help Ted Find His Fruit Popsicles!

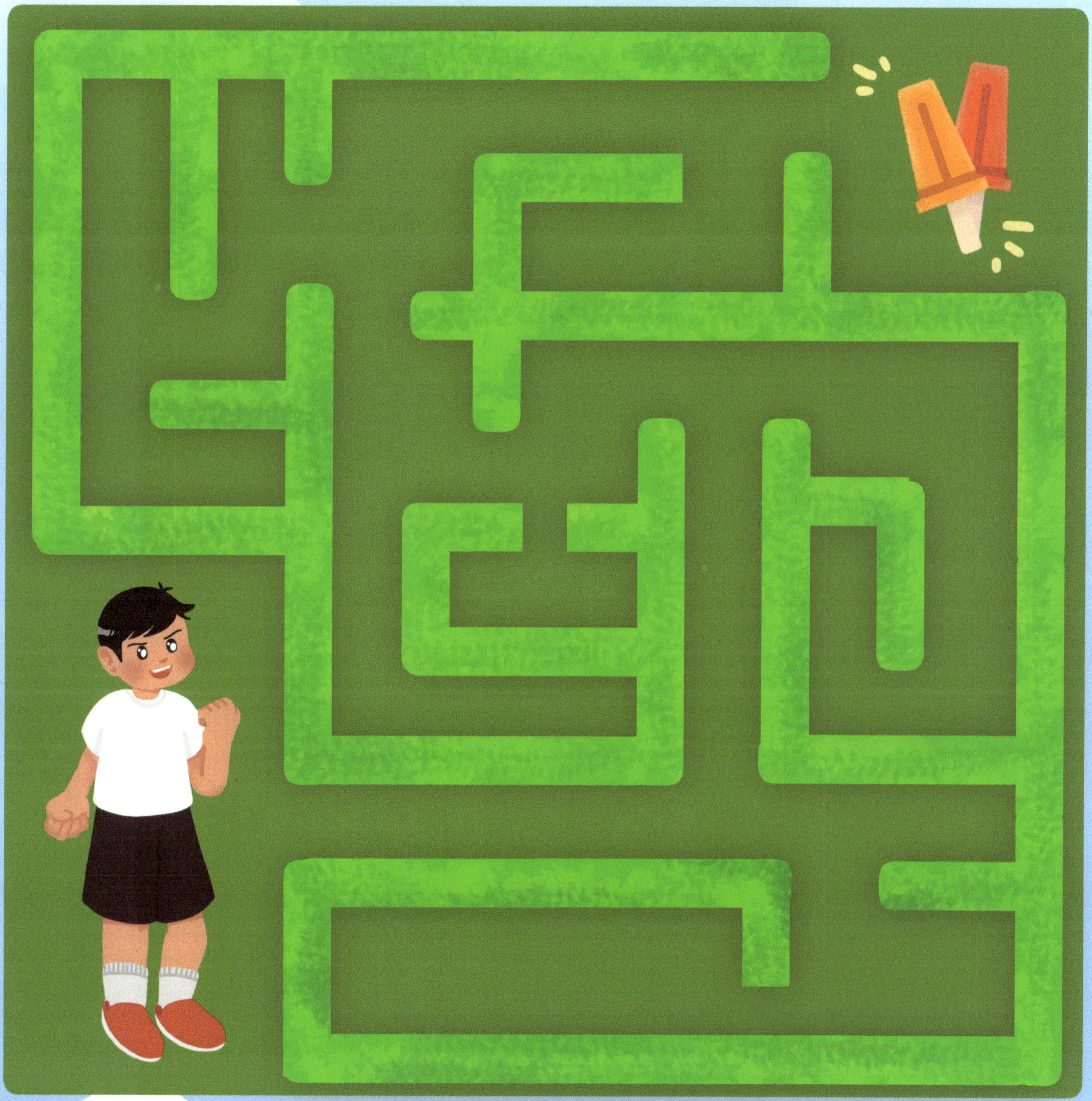

Find the Hidden Words! 

S	T	A	R	T	U	P	H	S
B	U	S	I	N	E	S	S	O
L	K	H	D	F	H	X	B	L
T	J	F	E	Q	B	Z	V	V
W	I	V	A	L	U	E	S	E
Y	H	Z	S	G	V	F	P	E
P	R	O	B	L	E	M	S	D

1. Solve

2. Business

3. Problems

4. Ideas

5. Startup

6. Values

Unjumble the Words!

Ppocisel	
Ifngish	
Sriutf	
Rvrei	
Ksabte	
Regdannig	

Spot the 5 Differences!

Help Ted Find His Fruit Popsicles!

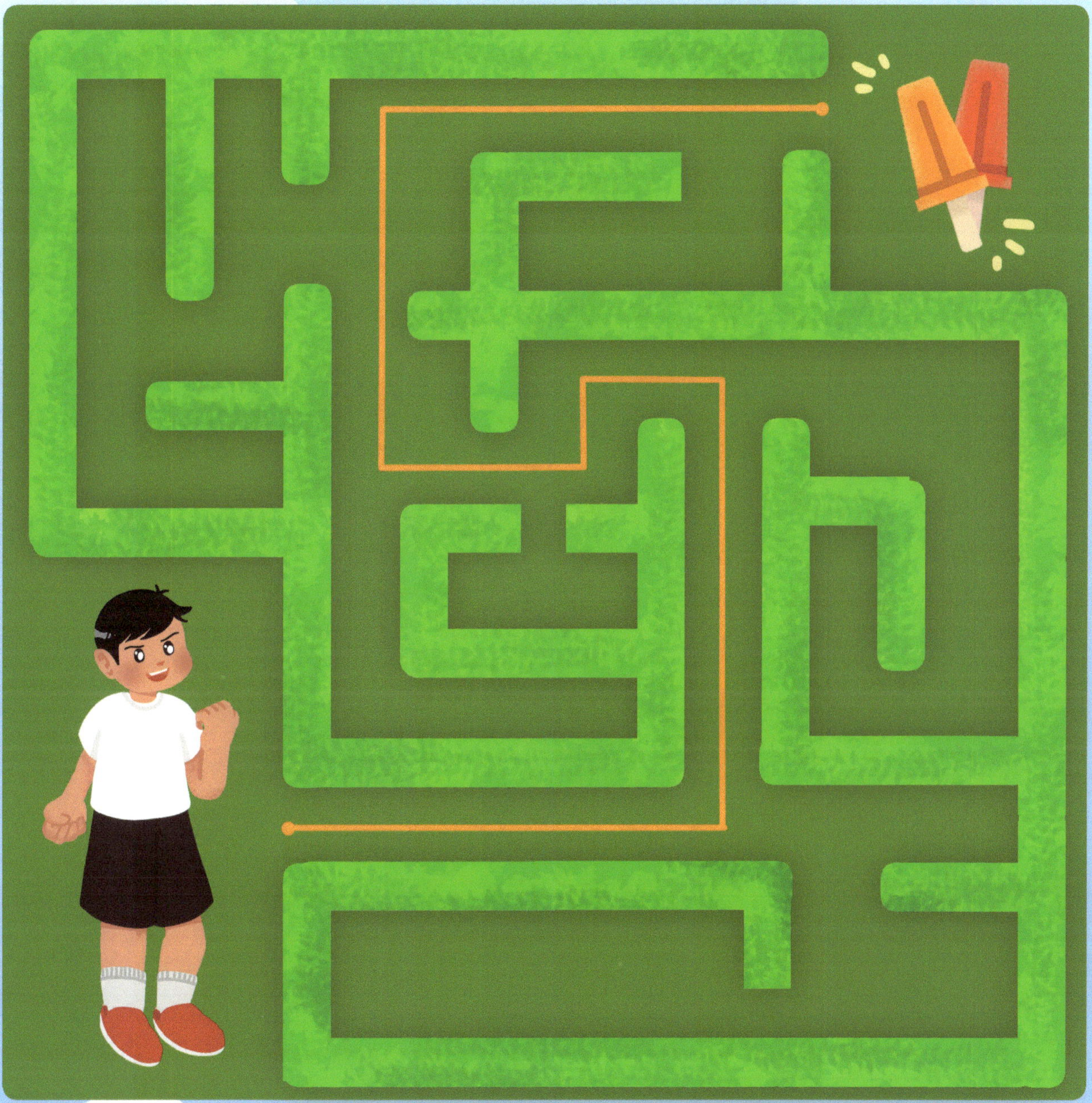

Find the Hidden Words!

S	T	A	R	T	U	P	H	S
B	U	S	I	N	E	S	S	O
L	K	H	D	F	H	X	B	L
T	J	F	E	Q	B	Z	V	V
W	I	V	A	L	U	E	S	E
Y	H	Z	S	G	V	F	P	E
P	R	O	B	L	E	M	S	D

1. Solve
2. Business
3. Problems
4. Ideas
5. Startup
6. Values

Unjumble the Words!

Ppocisel	Popsicle
Ifngish	Fishing
Sriutf	Fruits
Rvrei	River
Ksabte	Basket
Regdannig	Gardening

Ted Builds a Startup
Entrepreneurship
How You Can Be a Kidpreneur

www.ingramcontent.com/pod-product-compliance
Lightning Source LLC
Chambersburg PA
CBHW042008110726
48006CB00004B/1006